Vorname: _______________________________

Name: _______________________________

Anschrift: _______________________________

E-Mail: _______________________________

Telefonnummer: _______________________________

Seemeilen-Nachweise vor diesem Buch

Zeitraum: _______________________________

Zurückgelegte Seemeilen: _______________________________

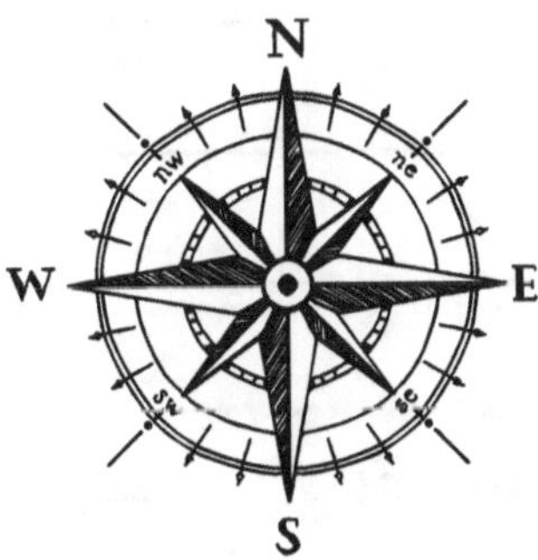

Übertrag

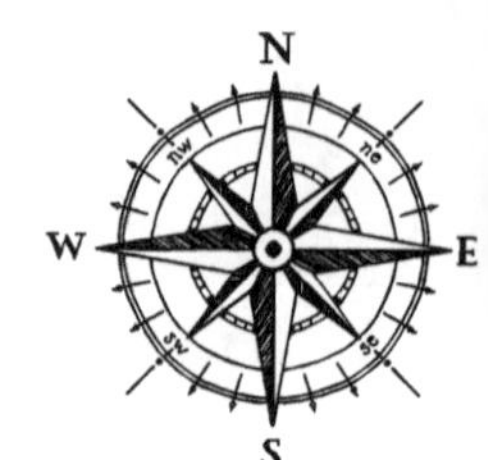

Seetage

Seemeilen

Lfd. Nr.	Fahrgebiet / Route	Seetage	Seemeilen

Summe ______________ ______________

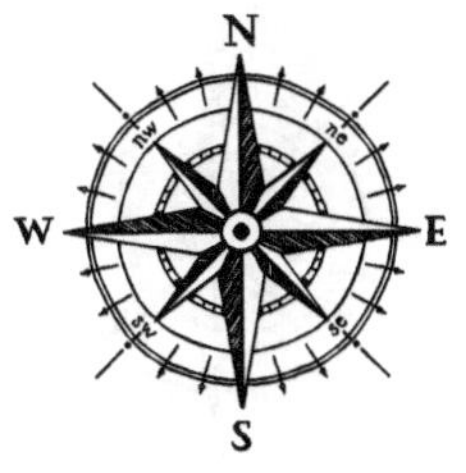

Übertrag

____
Seetage

____
Seemeilen

Lfd. Nr.	Fahrgebiet / Route	Seetage	Seemeilen

Summe _______________ _______________

Übertrag

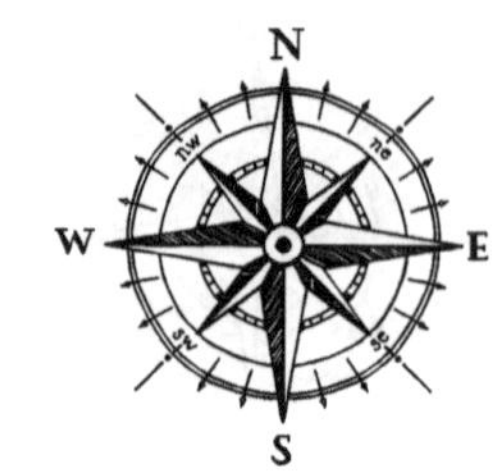

_______________   _______________
      Seetage   **Seemeilen**

Lfd. Nr.	Fahrgebiet / Route	Seetage	Seemeilen

Summe _______________   _______________

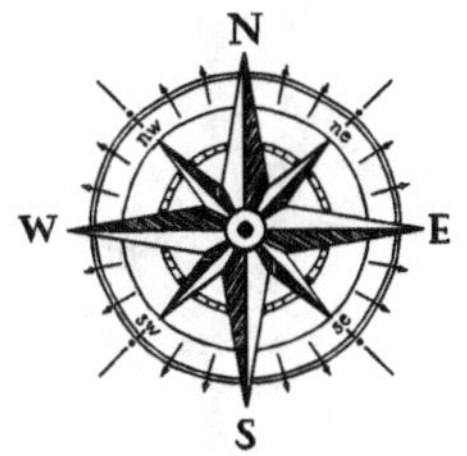

Übertrag

_______________________   _______________________

Seetage   **Seemeilen**

Lfd. Nr.	Fahrgebiet / Route	Seetage	Seemeilen

Summe _______________ _______________

Übertrag

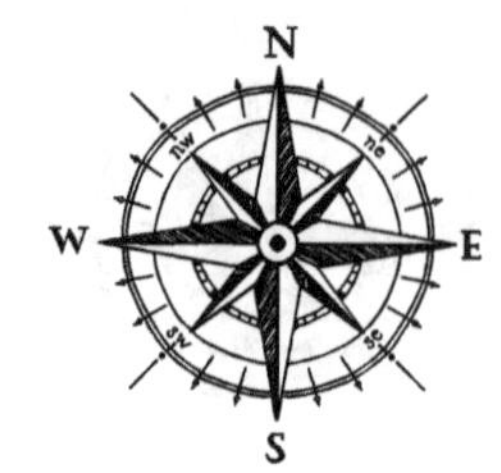

__________________________   __________________________

       Seetage   **Seemeilen**

Lfd. Nr.	Fahrgebiet / Route	Seetage	Seemeilen

Summe   __________________________   __________________________

Übertrag

__________________________   __________________________

Seetage   **Seemeilen**

Lfd. Nr.	Fahrgebiet / Route	Seetage	Seemeilen

Summe __________________   __________________

Übertrag

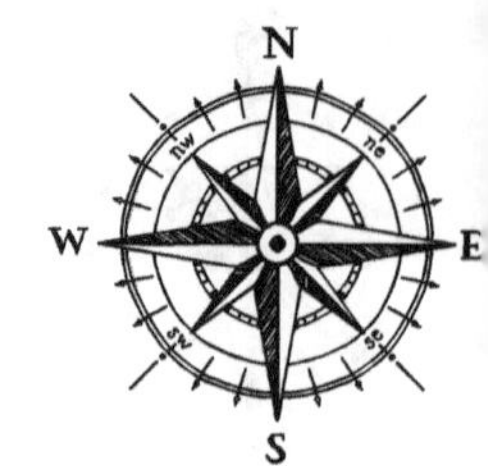

______________________   ______________________

Seetage   **Seemeilen**

Lfd. Nr.	Fahrgebiet / Route	Seetage	Seemeilen

Summe ______________________ ______________________

Übertrag

___________________________   ___________________________

Seetage   **Seemeilen**

Lfd. Nr.	Fahrgebiet / Route	Seetage	Seemeilen

Summe ___________________ ___________________

Übertrag

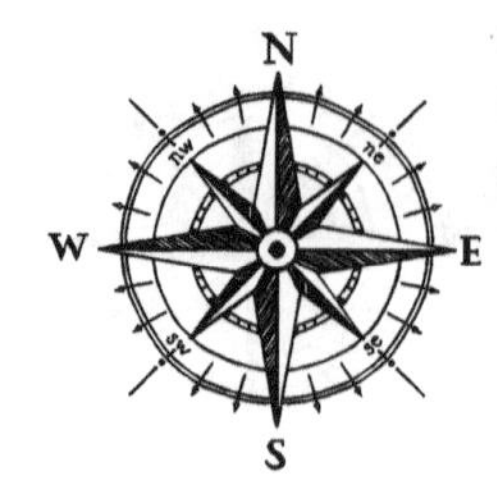

_______________   _______________

Seetage   **Seemeilen**

Lfd. Nr.	Fahrgebiet / Route	Seetage	Seemeilen

Summe _______________ _______________

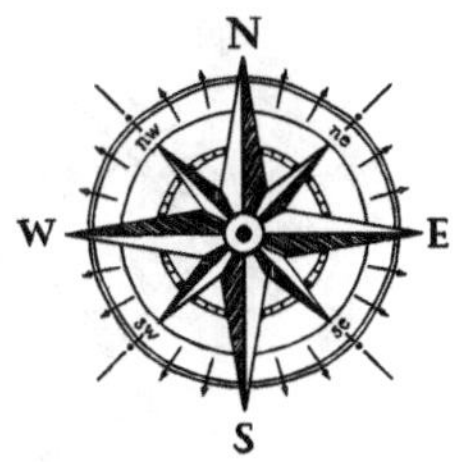

Übertrag

_________________________   _________________________

Seetage   **Seemeilen**

Lfd. Nr.	Fahrgebiet / Route	Seetage	Seemeilen

Summe   _________________   _________________

Übertrag

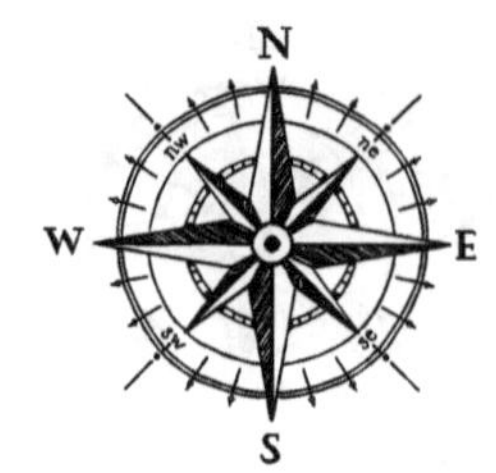

__________________ Seetage   __________________ Seemeilen

Lfd. Nr.	Fahrgebiet / Route	Seetage	Seemeilen

Summe __________________ __________________

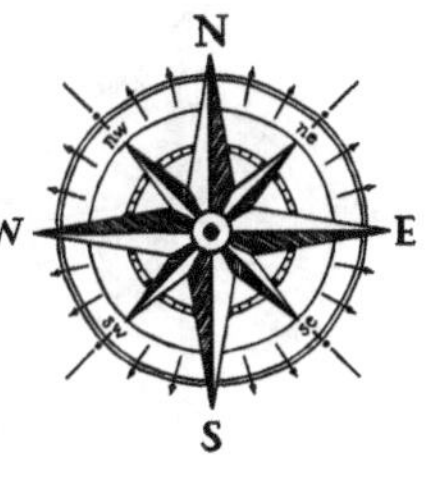

Übertrag

Seetage

Seemeilen

Lfd. Nr.	Fahrgebiet / Route	Seetage	Seemeilen

Summe ________ ________

Übertrag

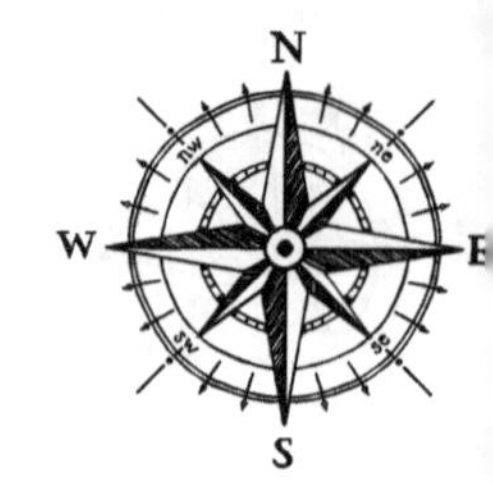

__________________   __________________

Seetage   **Seemeilen**

Lfd. Nr.	Fahrgebiet / Route	Seetage	Seemeilen

Summe   __________________   __________________

Übertrag

_____________________________ _____________________________
   Seetage   Seemeilen

Lfd. Nr.	Fahrgebiet / Route	Seetage	Seemeilen

Summe _____________________________ _____________________________

Übertrag

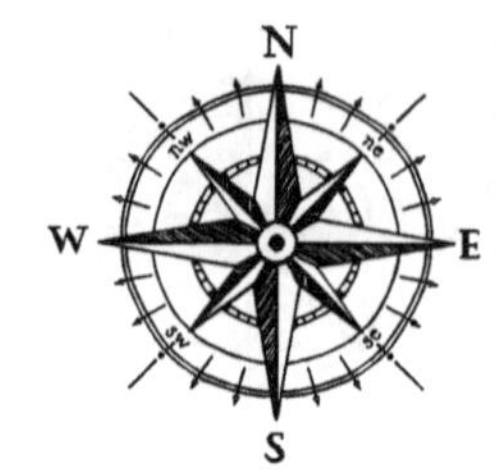

___________________   ___________________

Seetage   **Seemeilen**

Lfd. Nr.	Fahrgebiet / Route	Seetage	Seemeilen

Summe   ___________________   ___________________

Übertrag

__________________ __________________
Seetage   **Seemeilen**

Lfd. Nr.	Fahrgebiet / Route	Seetage	Seemeilen

Summe __________________ __________________

Übertrag

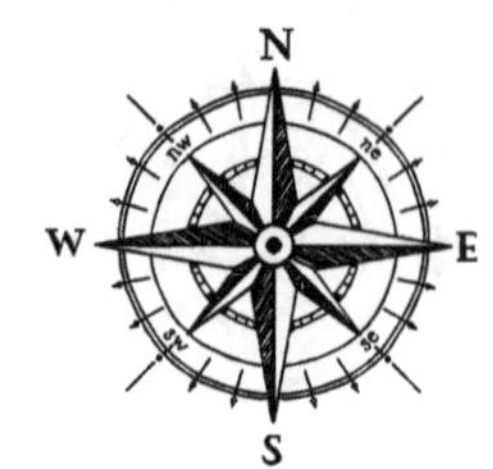

_________________________   _________________________
        Seetage   **Seemeilen**

Lfd. Nr.	Fahrgebiet / Route	Seetage	Seemeilen

Summe _________________ _________________

Übertrag

____
Seetage

____
Seemeilen

Lfd. Nr.	Fahrgebiet / Route	Seetage	Seemeilen

Summe _______________ _______________

Übertrag

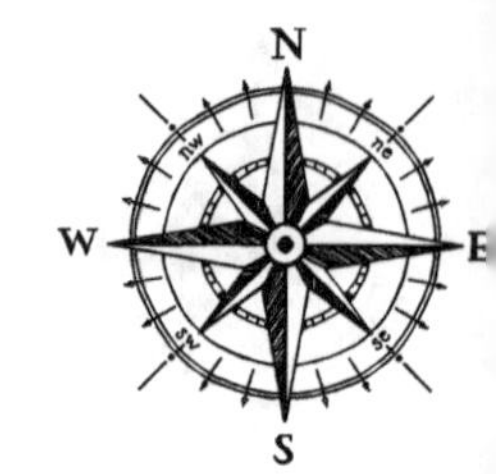

Seetage   **Seemeilen**

Lfd. Nr.	Fahrgebiet / Route	Seetage	Seemeilen

Summe

Übertrag

_________________________   _________________________

Seetage   **Seemeilen**

Lfd. Nr.	Fahrgebiet / Route	Seetage	Seemeilen

Summe _________________ __________

Übertrag

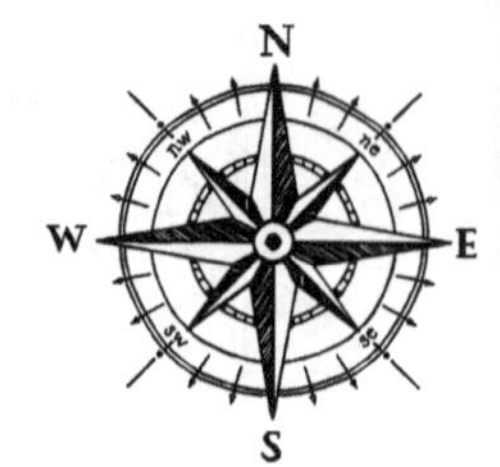

_______________   _______________

     Seetage   **Seemeilen**

Lfd. Nr.	Fahrgebiet / Route	Seetage	Seemeilen

Summe   _______________   _______________

Übertrag

Seetage

Seemeilen

Lfd. Nr.	Fahrgebiet / Route	Seetage	Seemeilen

Summe ______________ ______________

Übertrag

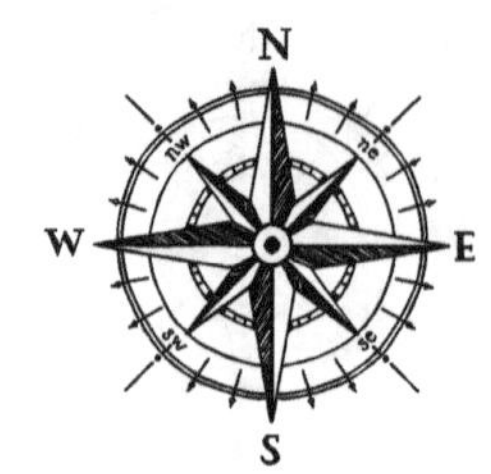

Seetage ________________________   **Seemeilen** ________________________

Lfd. Nr.	Fahrgebiet / Route	Seetage	Seemeilen

Summe ________________________   ________________________

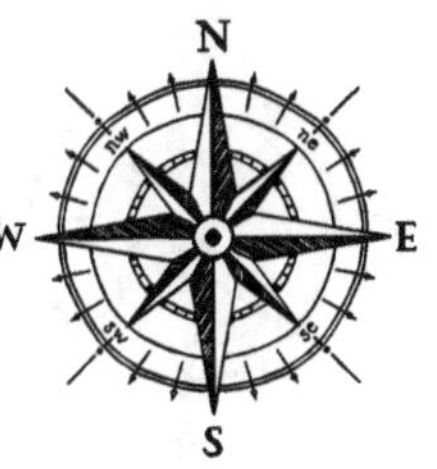

Übertrag

______________________ ______________________
Seetage   Seemeilen

Lfd. Nr.	Fahrgebiet / Route	Seetage	Seemeilen

Summe ______________________ ______________________

Übertrag

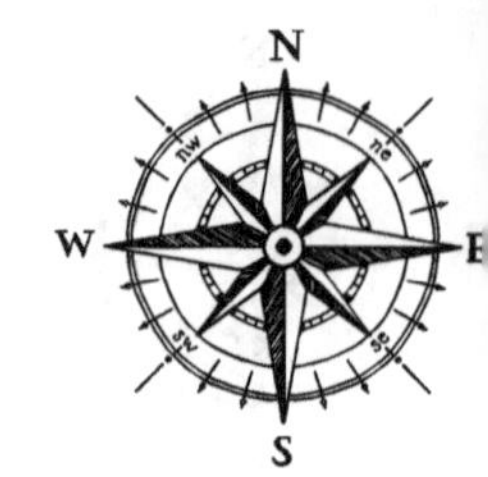

____________________ Seetage   ____________________ Seemeilen

Lfd. Nr.	Fahrgebiet / Route	Seetage	Seemeilen

Summe ____________________ ____________________

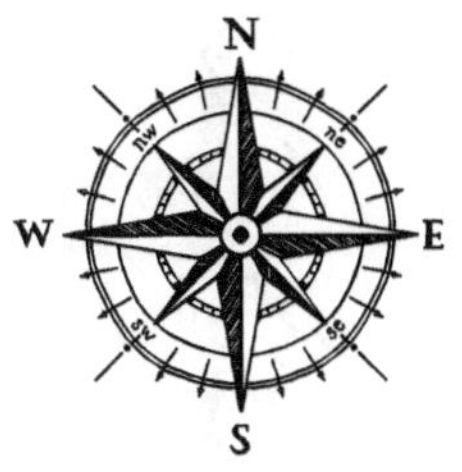

Übertrag

__________________________   __________________________
Seetage   **Seemeilen**

Lfd. Nr.	Fahrgebiet / Route	Seetage	Seemeilen

Summe __________________ __________________

Übertrag

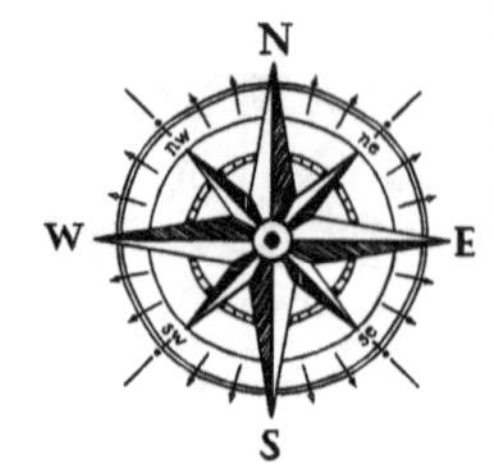

_________________________   _________________________

         Seetage   **Seemeilen**

Lfd. Nr.	Fahrgebiet / Route	Seetage	Seemeilen

Summe   _________________   _________________

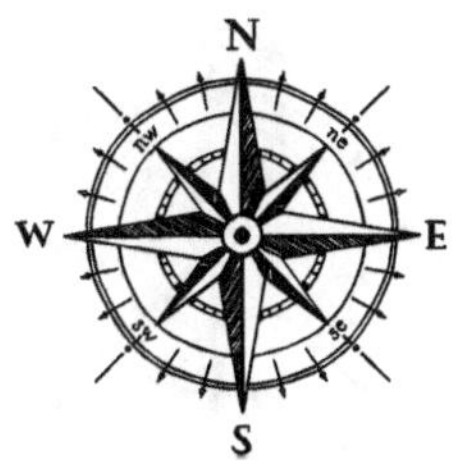

Übertrag

__________________________   __________________________
Seetage   **Seemeilen**

Lfd. Nr.	Fahrgebiet / Route	Seetage	Seemeilen

Summe __________________   __________________

Übertrag

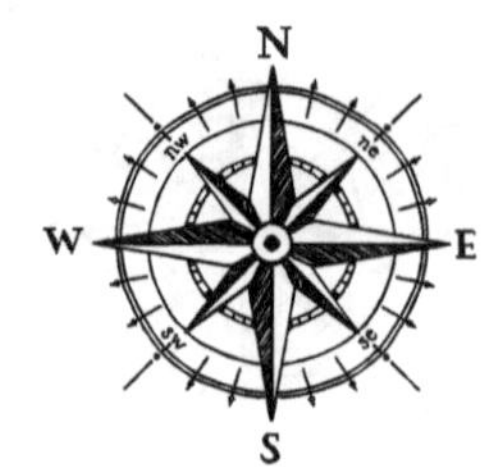

_________________   _________________

Seetage   **Seemeilen**

Lfd. Nr.	Fahrgebiet / Route	Seetage	Seemeilen

Summe   _________________ _________________

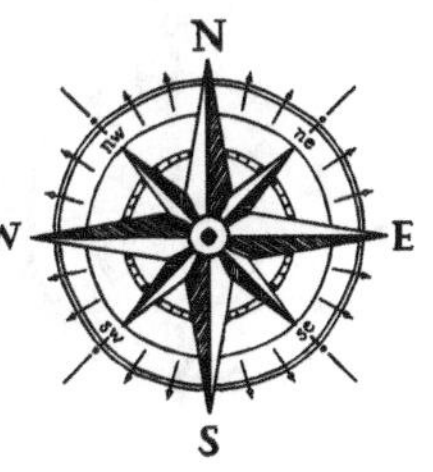

Übertrag

____
Seetage

____
Seemeilen

Lfd. Nr.	Fahrgebiet / Route	Seetage	Seemeilen

Summe _______________ _______________

Übertrag

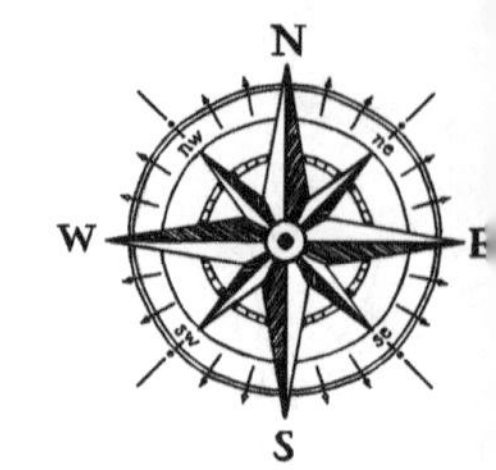

Seetage   **Seemeilen**

Lfd. Nr.	Fahrgebiet / Route	Seetage	Seemeilen

Summe

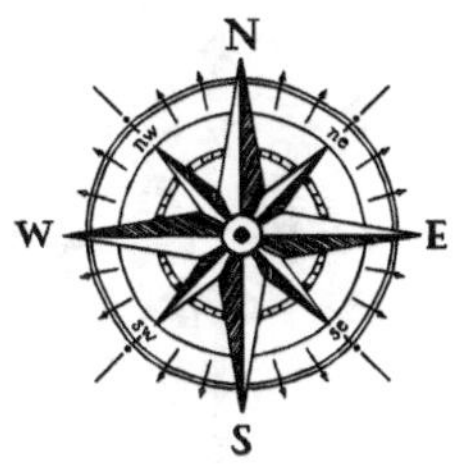

Übertrag

_________________________   _________________________

Seetage   **Seemeilen**

Lfd. Nr.	Fahrgebiet / Route	Seetage	Seemeilen

Summe   _________________   _________________

Übertrag

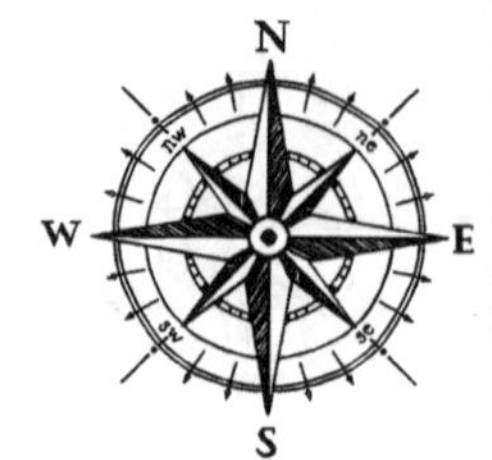

_____________________ _____________________
      Seetage   **Seemeilen**

Lfd. Nr.	Fahrgebiet / Route	Seetage	Seemeilen

Summe _____________________ _____________________

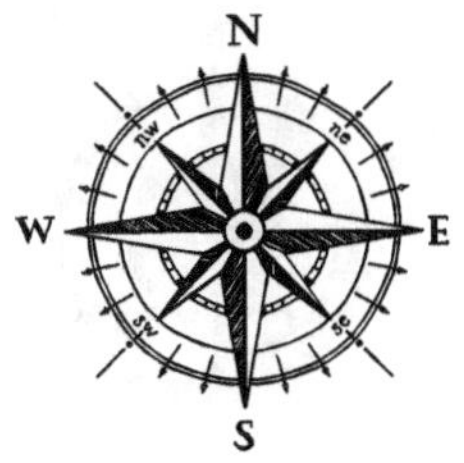

Übertrag

______________________   ______________________

Seetage   **Seemeilen**

Lfd. Nr.	Fahrgebiet / Route	Seetage	Seemeilen

Summe ______________________ ______________________

Übertrag

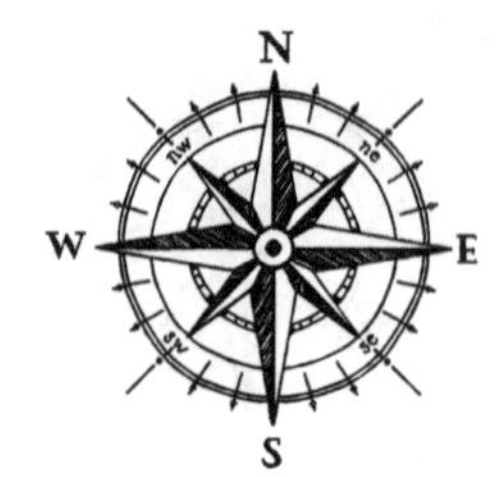

_______________   _______________
Seetage   **Seemeilen**

Lfd. Nr.	Fahrgebiet / Route	Seetage	Seemeilen

Summe _______________ _______________

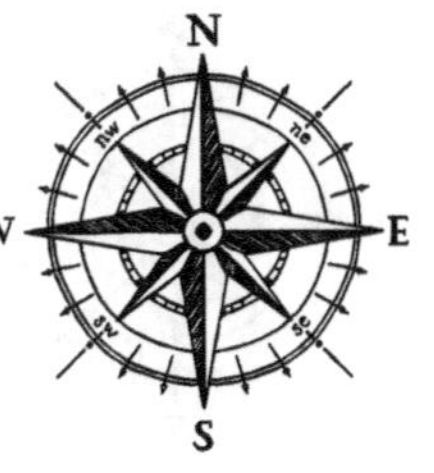

Übertrag

___________________   ___________________
Seetage   **Seemeilen**

Lfd. Nr.	Fahrgebiet / Route	Seetage	Seemeilen

Summe ___________________   ___________________

Übertrag

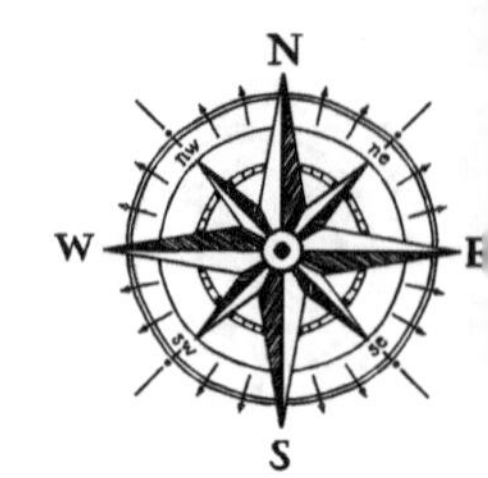

___________________   ___________________
Seetage   **Seemeilen**

Lfd. Nr.	Fahrgebiet / Route	Seetage	Seemeilen

Summe   ___________________   ___________________

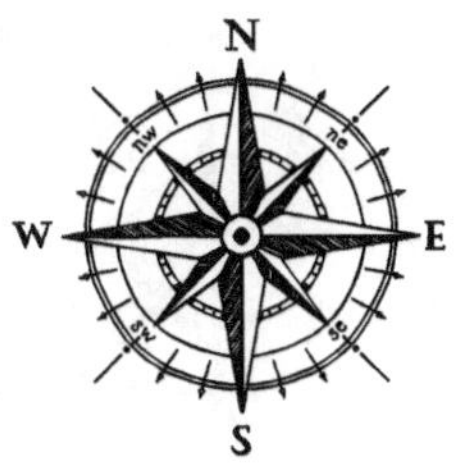

Übertrag

Seetage

Seemeilen

Lfd. Nr.	Fahrgebiet / Route	Seetage	Seemeilen

Summe

Übertrag

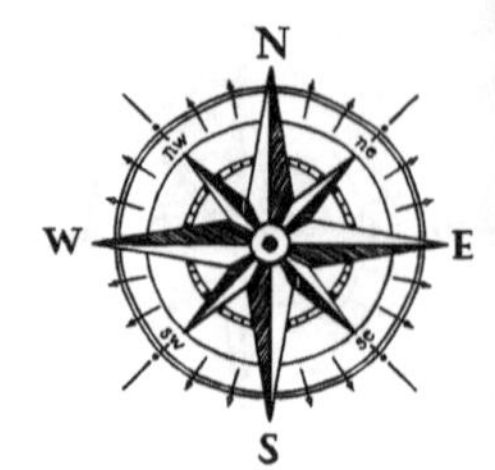

_________________________ Seetage

_________________________ Seemeilen

Lfd. Nr.	Fahrgebiet / Route	Seetage	Seemeilen

Summe _________________ _________________

Übertrag

_______________________   _______________________

Seetage   **Seemeilen**

Lfd. Nr.	Fahrgebiet / Route	Seetage	Seemeilen

Summe   _______________________   _______________________

Übertrag

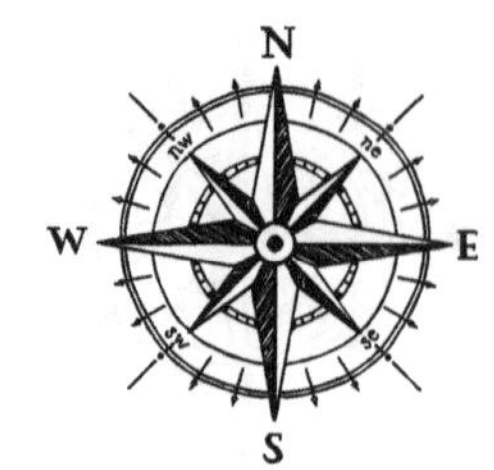

__________________ Seetage

__________________ Seemeilen

Lfd. Nr.	Fahrgebiet / Route	Seetage	Seemeilen

Summe __________ __________

Übertrag

__________________ __________________

Seetage **Seemeilen**

Lfd. Nr.	Fahrgebiet / Route	Seetage	Seemeilen

Summe __________ __________

Übertrag

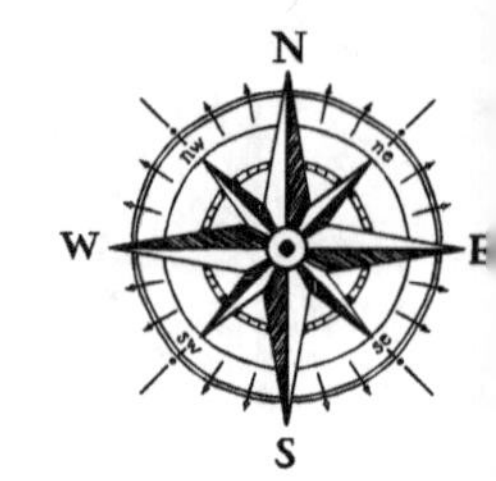

_______________   _______________
     Seetage   Seemeilen

Lfd. Nr.	Fahrgebiet / Route	Seetage	Seemeilen

Summe _______________ _______________

Übertrag

_______________________   _______________________

Seetage   **Seemeilen**

Lfd. Nr.	Fahrgebiet / Route	Seetage	Seemeilen

Summe   _______________   _______________

Übertrag

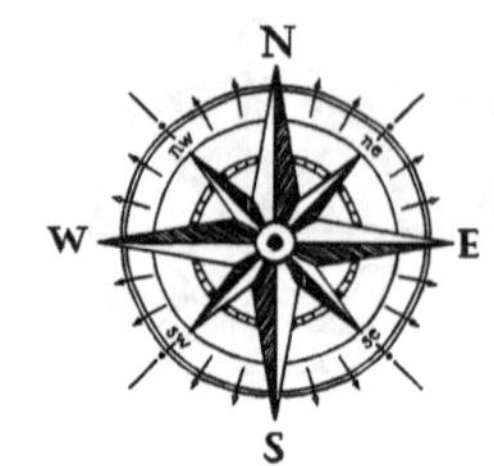

_______________ **Seetage**   _______________ **Seemeilen**

Lfd. Nr.	Fahrgebiet / Route	Seetage	Seemeilen

Summe _______________ _______________

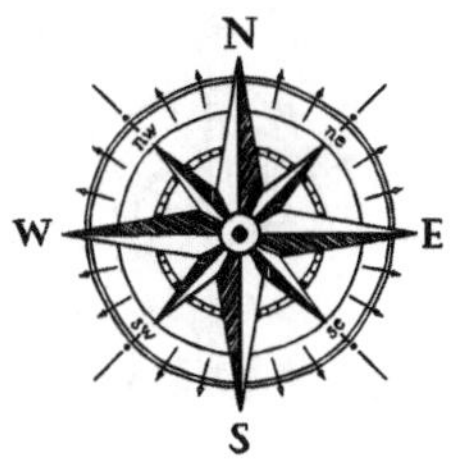

Übertrag

___________________   ___________________

Seetage   **Seemeilen**

Lfd. Nr.	Fahrgebiet / Route	Seetage	Seemeilen

Summe   ___________________   ___________________

Übertrag

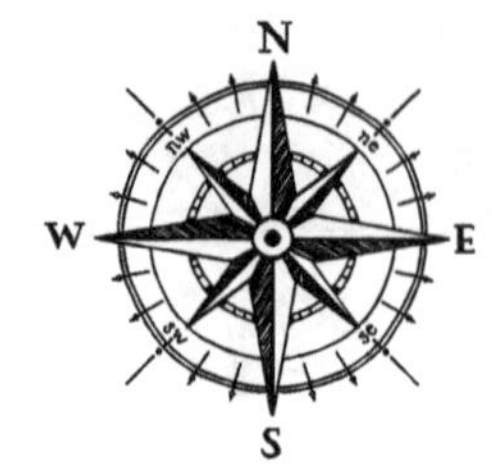

__________________   __________________

Seetage   **Seemeilen**

Lfd. Nr.	Fahrgebiet / Route	Seetage	Seemeilen

Summe __________________   __________________

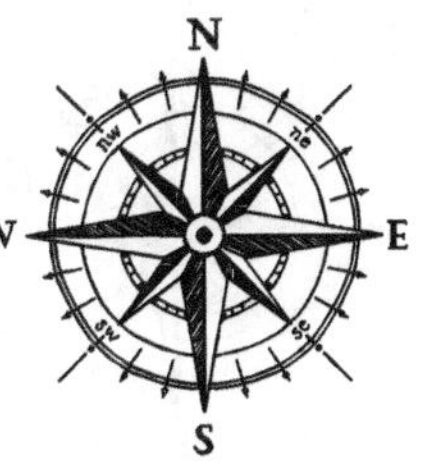

Übertrag

_________________________   _________________________
Seetage   Seemeilen

Lfd. Nr.	Fahrgebiet / Route	Seetage	Seemeilen

Summe _________________ _________________

Übertrag

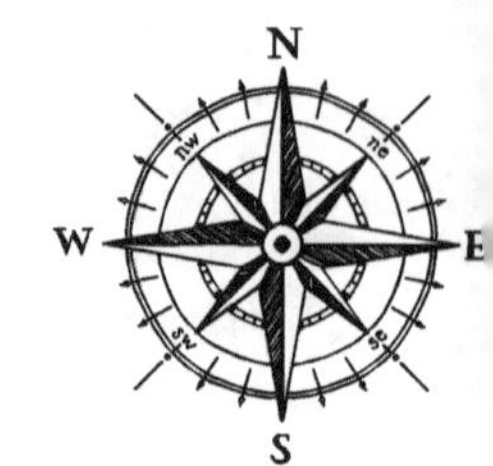

________________________ ________________________
 Seetage **Seemeilen**

Lfd. Nr.	Fahrgebiet / Route	Seetage	Seemeilen

Summe ________________ ________________

Übertrag

_________________________   _________________________

Seetage   Seemeilen

Lfd. Nr.	Fahrgebiet / Route	Seetage	Seemeilen

Summe _________________ _________________

Übertrag

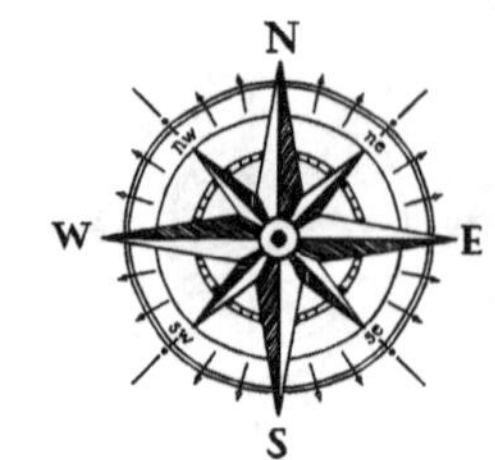

__________________________   __________________________

Seetage   **Seemeilen**

Lfd. Nr.	Fahrgebiet / Route	Seetage	Seemeilen

Summe   __________________   __________________

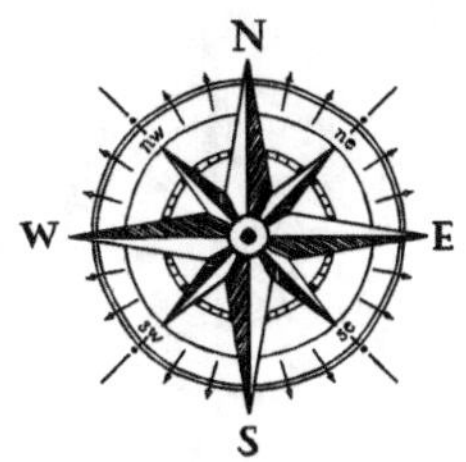

Übertrag

____
Seetage

____
Seemeilen

Lfd. Nr.	Fahrgebiet / Route	Seetage	Seemeilen

Summe __________________ __________________

Übertrag

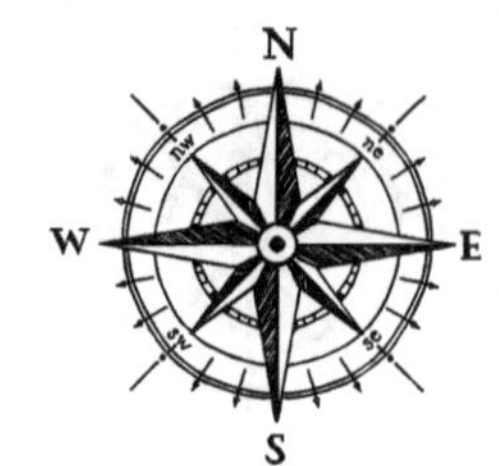

__________________ Seetage   __________________ Seemeilen

Lfd. Nr.	Fahrgebiet / Route	Seetage	Seemeilen

Summe __________________ __________________

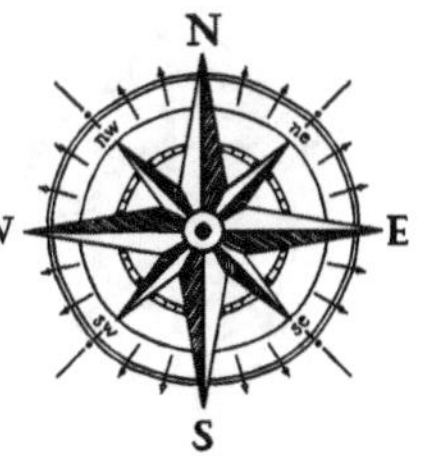

Übertrag

_________________________   _________________________

       Seetage   **Seemeilen**

Lfd. Nr.	Fahrgebiet / Route	Seetage	Seemeilen

Summe _________________________ _________________________

Übertrag

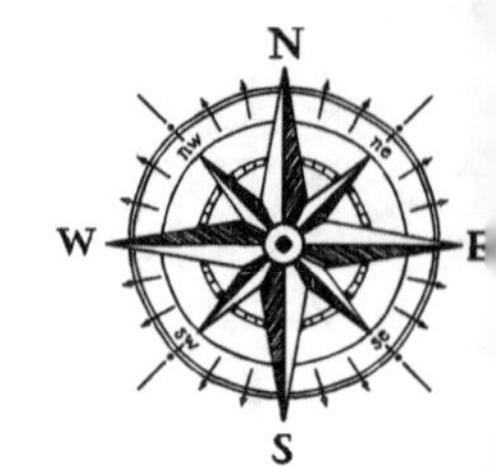

______________________   ______________________

Seetage   **Seemeilen**

Lfd. Nr.	Fahrgebiet / Route	Seetage	Seemeilen

Summe   ______________   ______________

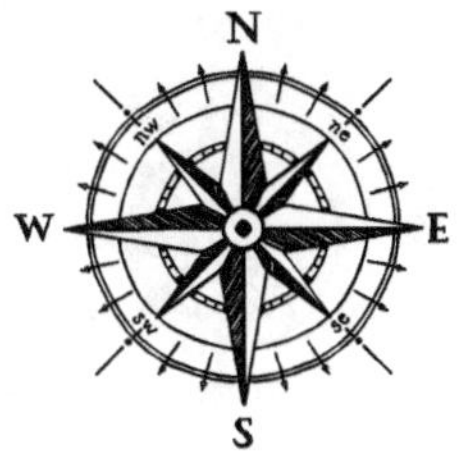

Übertrag

__________________________   __________________________

       Seetage   **Seemeilen**

Lfd. Nr.	Fahrgebiet / Route	Seetage	Seemeilen

Summe __________________ __________________

Übertrag

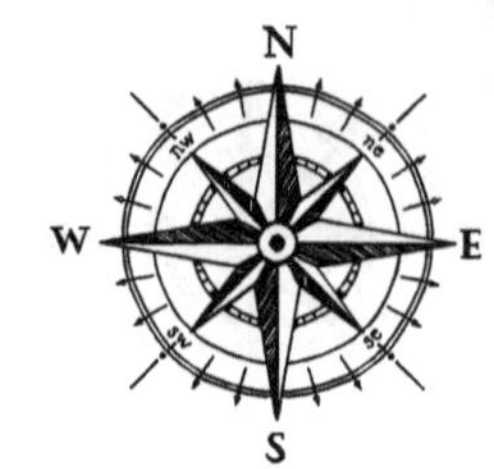

______________________   ______________________

Seetage   **Seemeilen**

Lfd. Nr.	Fahrgebiet / Route	Seetage	Seemeilen

Summe   ______________________   ______________________

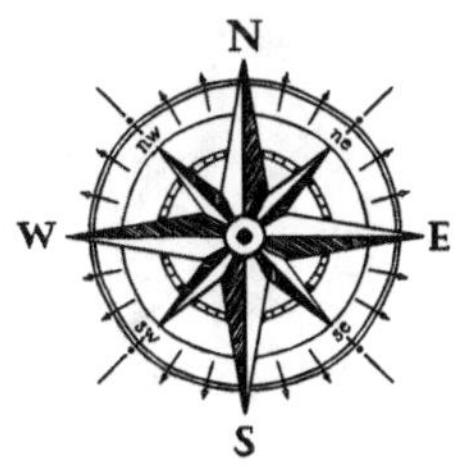

Übertrag

Seetage

Seemeilen

Lfd. Nr.	Fahrgebiet / Route	Seetage	Seemeilen

Summe _____________ _____________

Übertrag

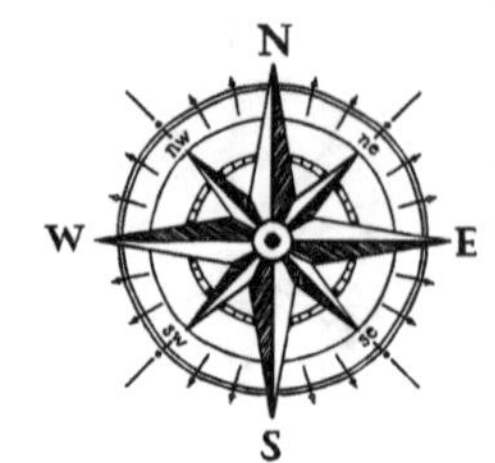

________________________   ________________________

Seetage   **Seemeilen**

Lfd. Nr.	Fahrgebiet / Route	Seetage	Seemeilen

Summe   ________________________   ________________________

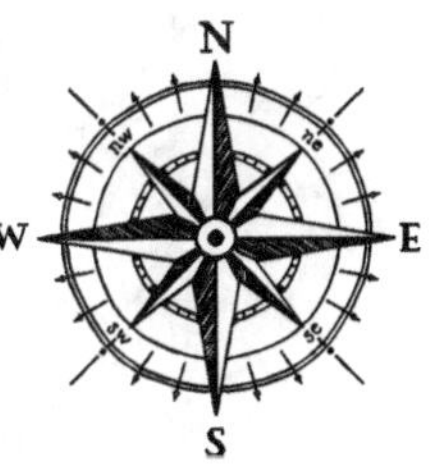

Übertrag

__________________________ __________________________
Seetage   Seemeilen

Lfd. Nr.	Fahrgebiet / Route	Seetage	Seemeilen

Summe __________________ __________________

Übertrag

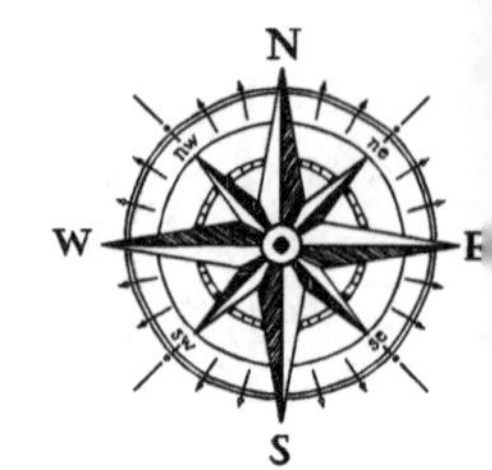

___________________   ___________________

    Seetage   **Seemeilen**

Lfd. Nr.	Fahrgebiet / Route	Seetage	Seemeilen

Summe ___________________ ___________________

Übertrag

_______________________   _______________________
          Seetage   **Seemeilen**

Lfd. Nr.	Fahrgebiet / Route	Seetage	Seemeilen

Summe   _______________   _______________

Übertrag

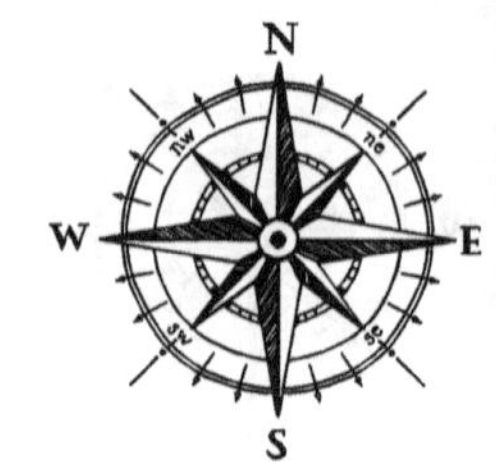

__________________________   __________________________

     Seetage   Seemeilen

Lfd. Nr.	Fahrgebiet / Route	Seetage	Seemeilen

Summe   __________________________   __________________________

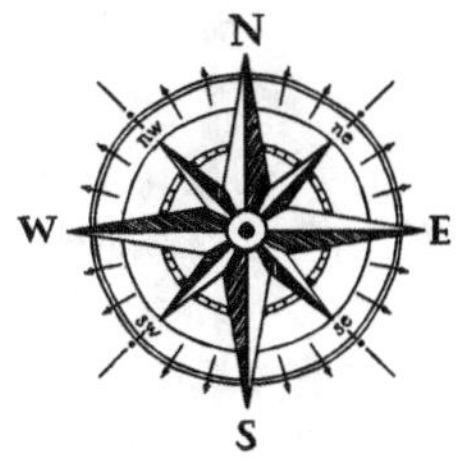

Übertrag

__________________   __________________

Seetage   **Seemeilen**

Lfd. Nr.	Fahrgebiet / Route	Seetage	Seemeilen

Summe _______________ _______________

Übertrag

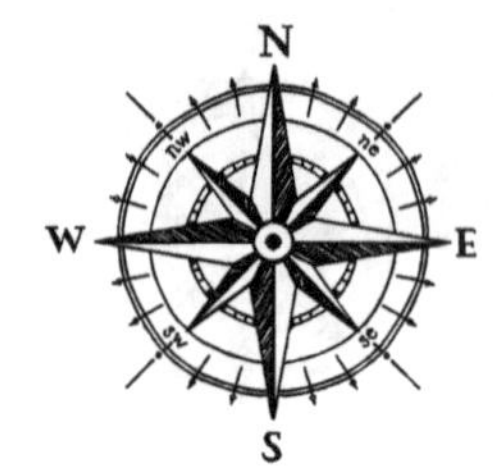

_______________ _______________
Seetage   Seemeilen

Lfd. Nr.	Fahrgebiet / Route	Seetage	Seemeilen

Summe _______________ _______________

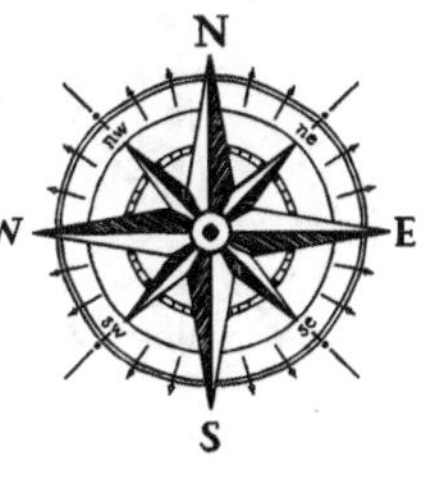

Übertrag

____
Seetage

____
Seemeilen

Lfd. Nr.	Fahrgebiet / Route	Seetage	Seemeilen

Summe _____________ _____________

Übertrag

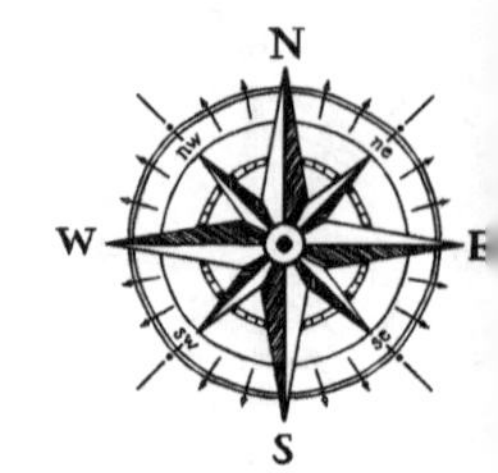

__________________   __________________
Seetage   **Seemeilen**

Lfd. Nr.	Fahrgebiet / Route	Seetage	Seemeilen

Summe _______________ _______________

Übertrag

______________________   ______________________
Seetage   **Seemeilen**

Lfd. Nr.	Fahrgebiet / Route	Seetage	Seemeilen

Summe ______________________   ______________________

Übertrag

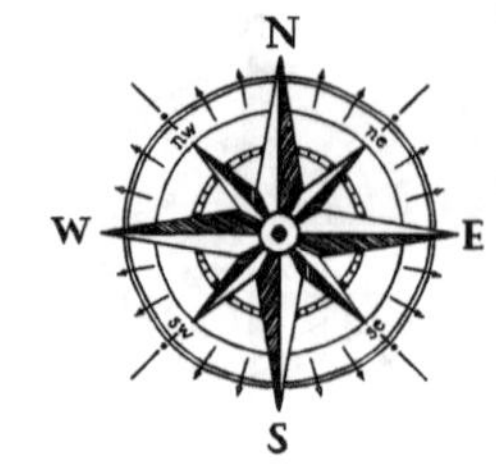

__________________________   __________________________

        Seetage   Seemeilen

Lfd. Nr.	Fahrgebiet / Route	Seetage	Seemeilen

Summe __________________ __________________

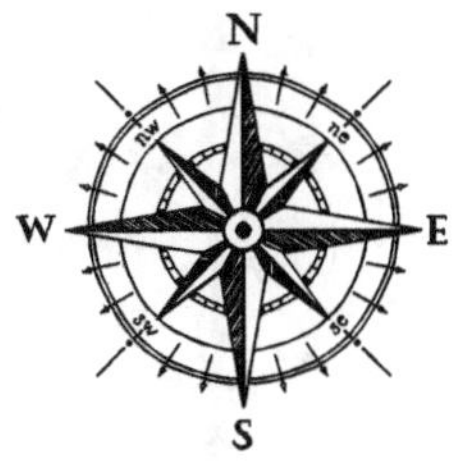

Übertrag

________________________   ________________________

Seetage   **Seemeilen**

Lfd. Nr.	Fahrgebiet / Route	Seetage	Seemeilen

Summe ________________________   ________________________

Übertrag

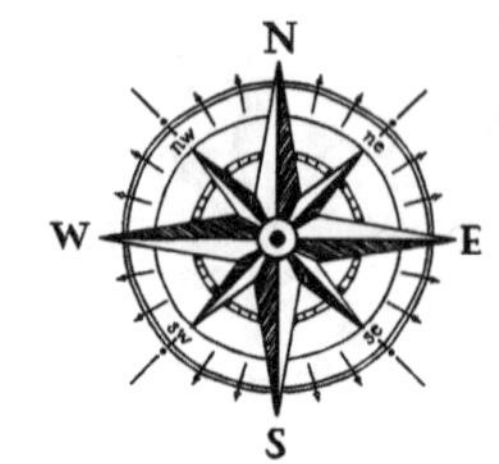

______________   ______________
Seetage   **Seemeilen**

Lfd. Nr.	Fahrgebiet / Route	Seetage	Seemeilen

Summe   ______________   ______________

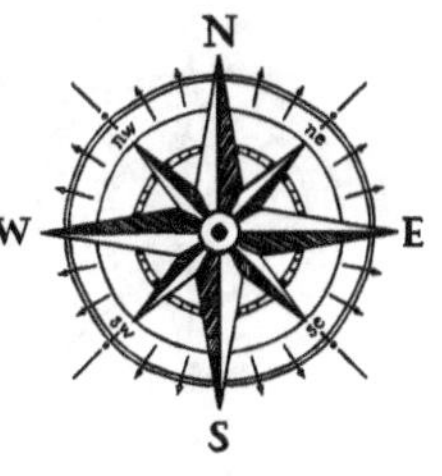

Übertrag

_________________________   _________________________

Seetage   **Seemeilen**

Lfd. Nr.	Fahrgebiet / Route	Seetage	Seemeilen

Summe   _________________   _________________

Übertrag

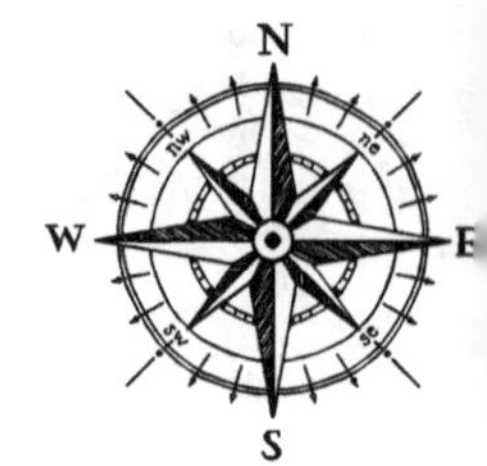

<u>   </u> **Seetage**   <u>   </u> **Seemeilen**

Lfd. Nr.	Fahrgebiet / Route	Seetage	Seemeilen

Summe _________________ _________________

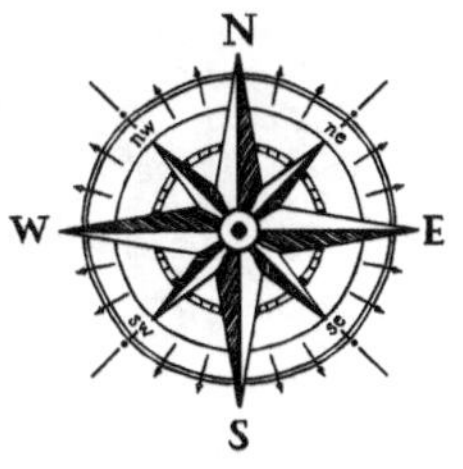

Übertrag

____
Seetage

____
Seemeilen

Lfd. Nr.	Fahrgebiet / Route	Seetage	Seemeilen

Summe _______________ _______________

Übertrag

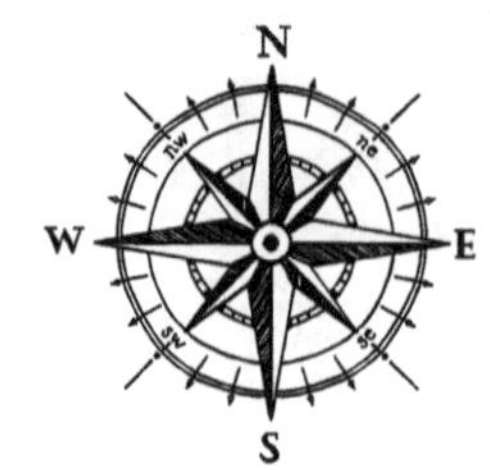

_______________   _______________

Seetage   **Seemeilen**

Lfd. Nr.	Fahrgebiet / Route	Seetage	Seemeilen

Summe   _______________   _______________

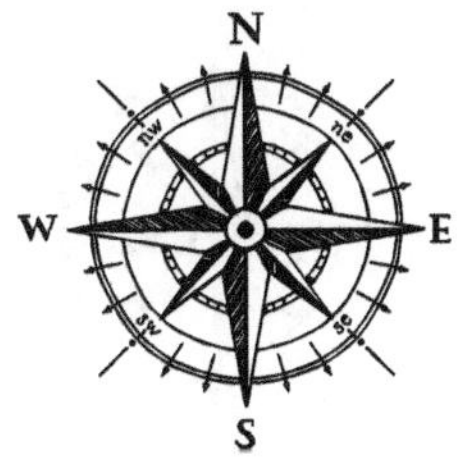

Übertrag

____
Seetage

____
Seemeilen

Lfd. Nr.	Fahrgebiet / Route	Seetage	Seemeilen

Summe ___________________ ___________________

Übertrag

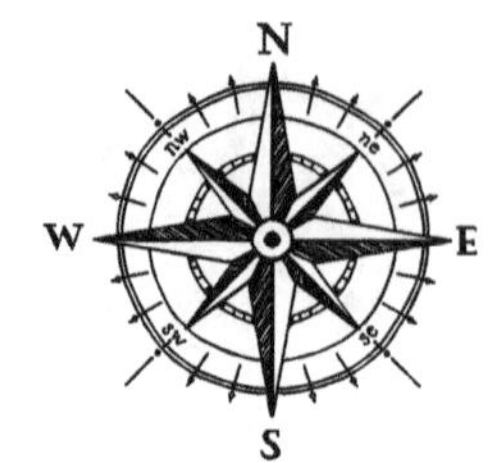

__________________   __________________
     Seetage   Seemeilen

Lfd. Nr.	Fahrgebiet / Route	Seetage	Seemeilen

Summe   __________________   __________________

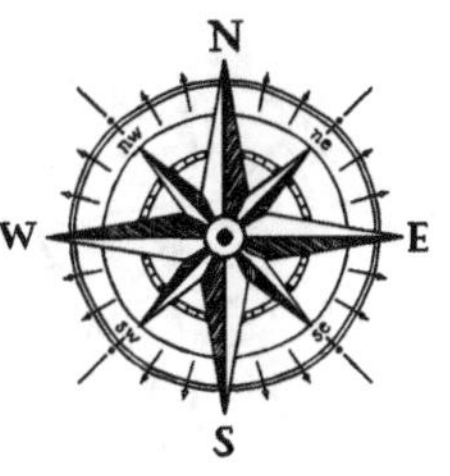

Übertrag

_______________________   _______________________
Seetage   **Seemeilen**

Lfd. Nr.	Fahrgebiet / Route	Seetage	Seemeilen

Summe _______________________ _______________________

Übertrag

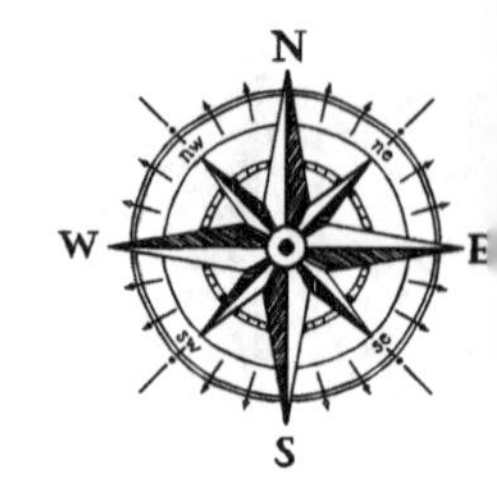

_____________________ _____________________
Seetage   **Seemeilen**

Lfd. Nr.	Fahrgebiet / Route	Seetage	Seemeilen

Summe _____________________ _____________________

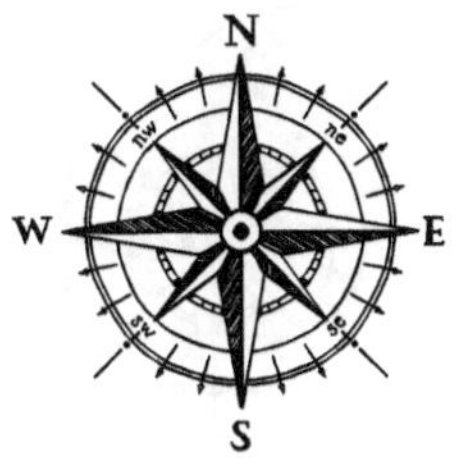

Übertrag

_________________   _________________

Seetage   **Seemeilen**

Lfd. Nr.	Fahrgebiet / Route	Seetage	Seemeilen

Summe _________________ _________________

Übertrag

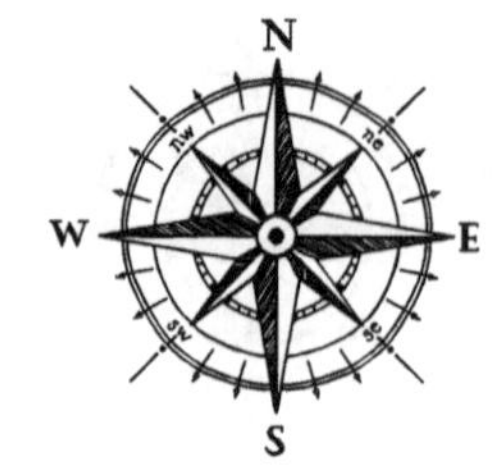

—————————————————   —————————————————

      Seetage   **Seemeilen**

Lfd. Nr.	Fahrgebiet / Route	Seetage	Seemeilen

Summe —————————————   —————————————

Übertrag

__________________   __________________

Seetage   **Seemeilen**

Lfd. Nr.	Fahrgebiet / Route	Seetage	Seemeilen

Summe __________________   __________________

Übertrag

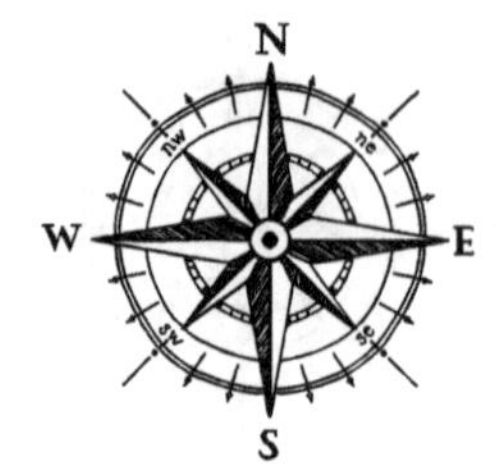

Seetage

Seemeilen

Lfd. Nr.	Fahrgebiet / Route	Seetage	Seemeilen

Summe ———————— ————————

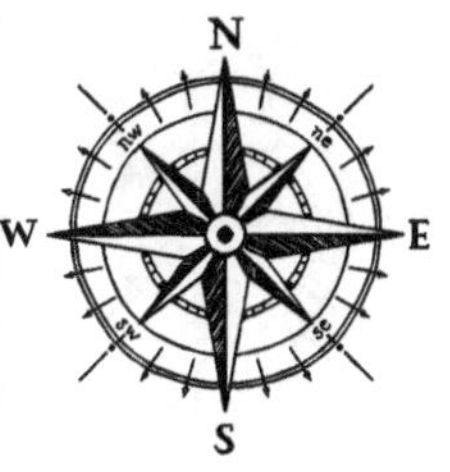

Übertrag

__________________________   __________________________

Seetage   **Seemeilen**

Lfd. Nr.	Fahrgebiet / Route	Seetage	Seemeilen

Summe __________________ __________________

Übertrag

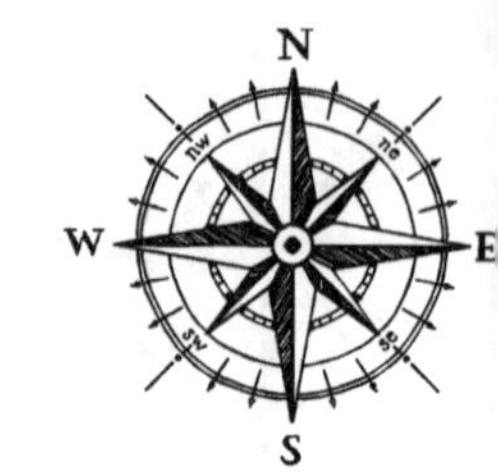

_______________   _______________

Seetage   **Seemeilen**

Lfd. Nr.	Fahrgebiet / Route	Seetage	Seemeilen

Summe   _______________   _______________

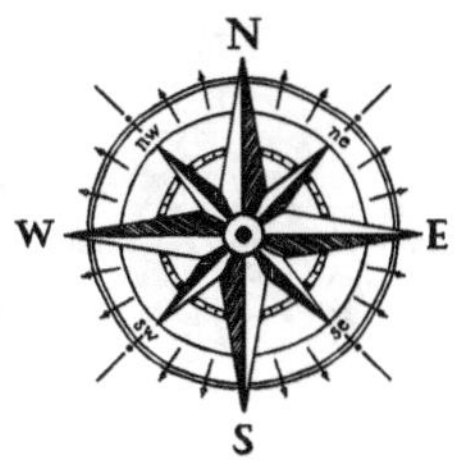

Übertrag

____
Seetage

____
Seemeilen

Lfd. Nr.	Fahrgebiet / Route	Seetage	Seemeilen

Summe _____________ _____________

Übertrag

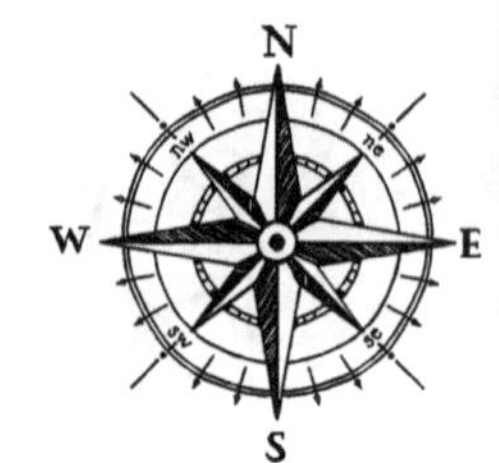

Seetage   **Seemeilen**

Lfd. Nr.	Fahrgebiet / Route	Seetage	Seemeilen

Summe ________________ ________________

Übertrag

____________________ ____________________

Seetage **Seemeilen**

Lfd. Nr.	Fahrgebiet / Route	Seetage	Seemeilen

Summe ____________________ ____________________

Übertrag

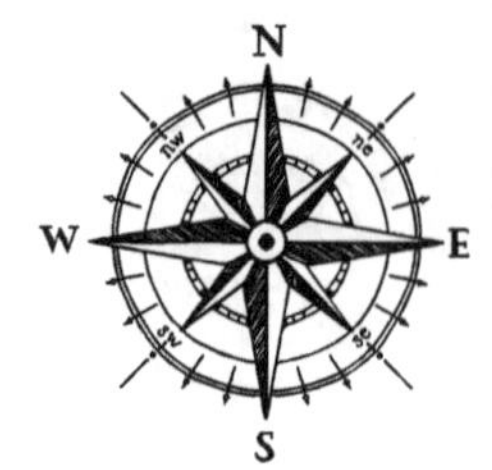

__________________   Seetage   __________________   Seemeilen

Lfd. Nr.	Fahrgebiet / Route	Seetage	Seemeilen

Summe   __________________   __________________

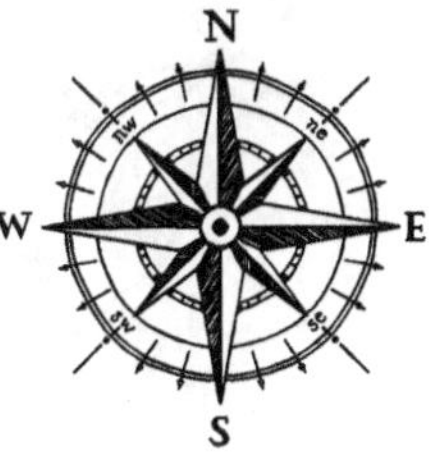

Übertrag

_________________________   _________________________
Seetage   **Seemeilen**

Lfd. Nr.	Fahrgebiet / Route	Seetage	Seemeilen

Summe _________________ _________________

Übertrag

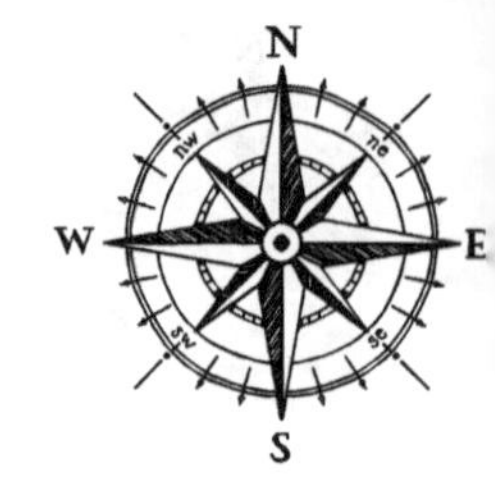

__________________ __________________

Seetage **Seemeilen**

Lfd. Nr.	Fahrgebiet / Route	Seetage	Seemeilen

Summe __________________ __________________

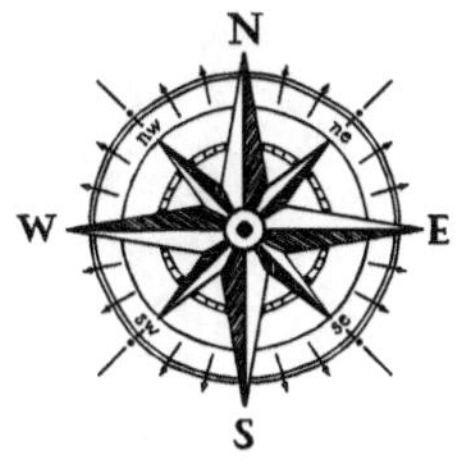

Übertrag

Seetage	Seemeilen

Lfd. Nr.	Fahrgebiet / Route	Seetage	Seemeilen

Summe ———————— ————————

Übertrag

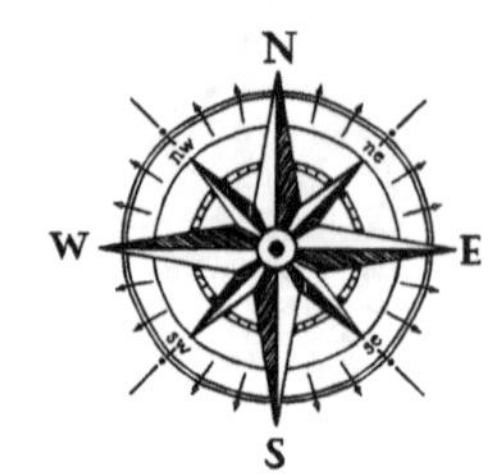

__________________   __________________
       Seetage   Seemeilen

Lfd. Nr.	Fahrgebiet / Route	Seetage	Seemeilen

Summe __________________   __________________

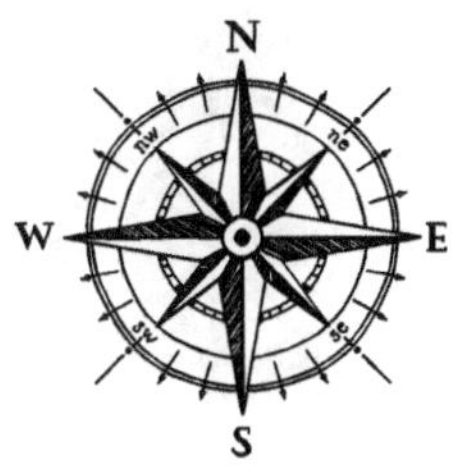

Übertrag

_________________________   _________________________

Seetage   **Seemeilen**

Lfd. Nr.	Fahrgebiet / Route	Seetage	Seemeilen

Summe   _________________   _________________

Übertrag

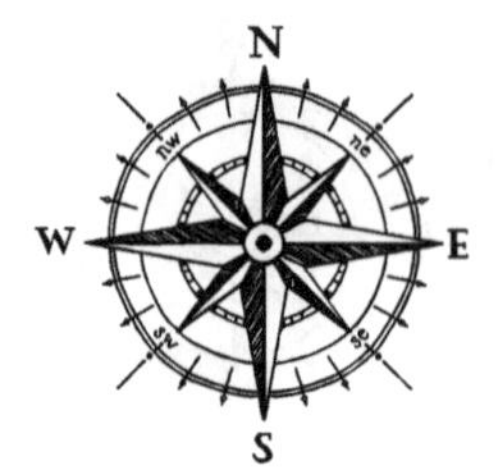

_____________________   _____________________

Seetage   **Seemeilen**

Lfd. Nr.	Fahrgebiet / Route	Seetage	Seemeilen

Summe   _____________________   _____________________

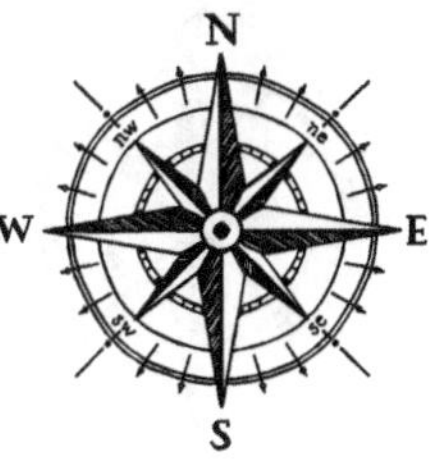

Übertrag

_______________________   _______________________
Seetage   **Seemeilen**

Lfd. Nr.	Fahrgebiet / Route	Seetage	Seemeilen

Summe _______________ _______________

Übertrag

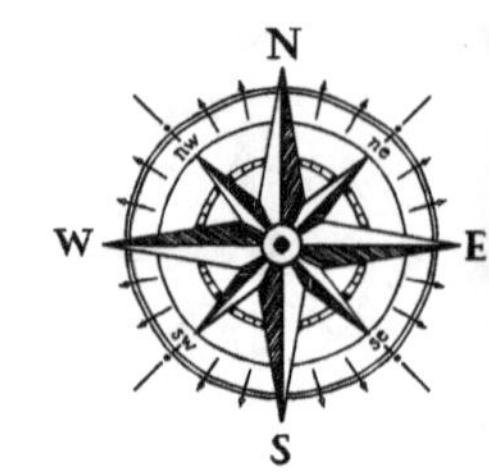

Seetage **Seemeilen**.

Lfd. Nr.	Fahrgebiet / Route	Seetage	Seemeilen

Summe ——————— ———————

Übertrag

______________________   ______________________

Seetage   **Seemeilen**

Lfd. Nr.	Fahrgebiet / Route	Seetage	Seemeilen

Summe   ______________________   ______________________

Übertrag

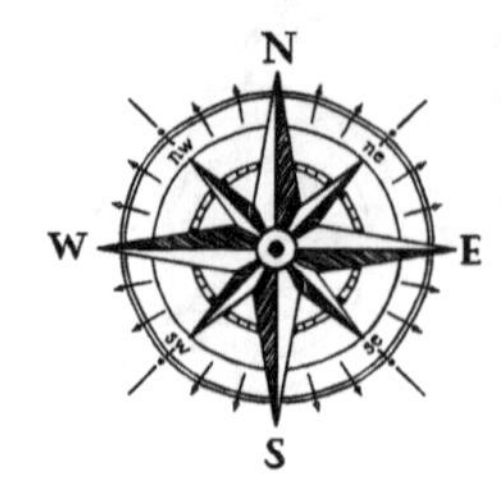

__________________ Seetage   __________________ Seemeilen

Lfd. Nr.	Fahrgebiet / Route	Seetage	Seemeilen

Summe __________________ __________________

Übertrag

______________________   ______________________

Seetage   **Seemeilen**

Lfd. Nr.	Fahrgebiet / Route	Seetage	Seemeilen

Summe ______________________ ______________________

Übertrag

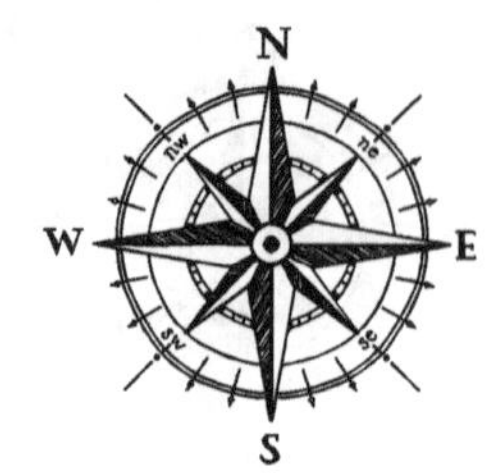

Seetage   **Seemeilen**

Lfd. Nr.	Fahrgebiet / Route	Seetage	Seemeilen

Summe

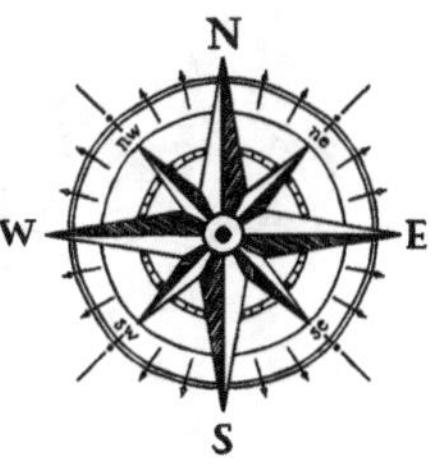

Übertrag

_________________________   _________________________

Seetage   **Seemeilen**

Lfd. Nr.	Fahrgebiet / Route	Seetage	Seemeilen

Summe _________________ _________________

Übertrag

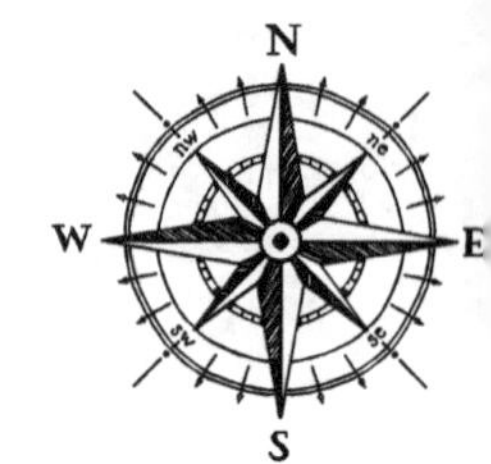

__________________   __________________
      Seetage   **Seemeilen**

Lfd. Nr.	Fahrgebiet / Route	Seetage	Seemeilen

Summe __________________ __________________

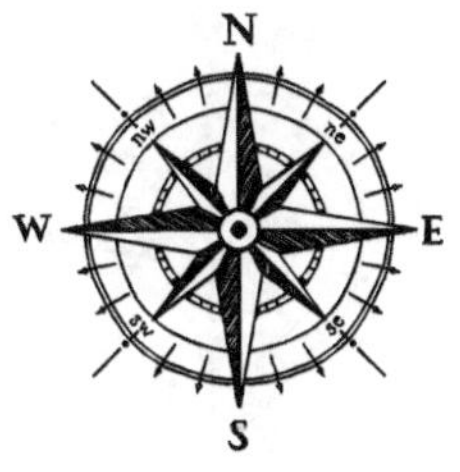

Übertrag

______________________   ______________________

Seetage   **Seemeilen**

Lfd. Nr.	Fahrgebiet / Route	Seetage	Seemeilen

Summe ______________________ ______________________

Übertrag

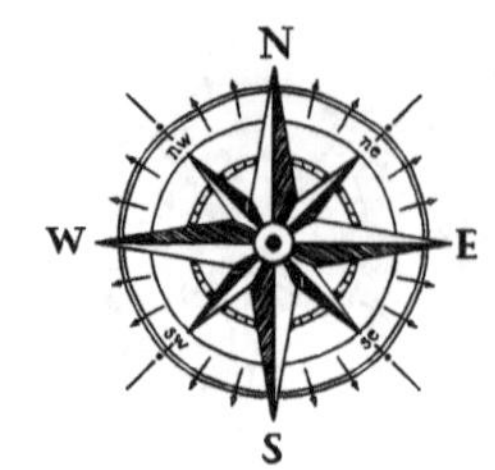

____
Seetage

____
Seemeilen

Lfd. Nr.	Fahrgebiet / Route	Seetage	Seemeilen

Summe _____________ _____________

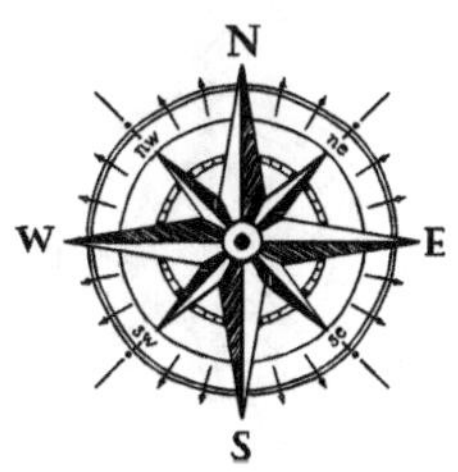

Übertrag

_______________________   _______________________
       Seetage   **Seemeilen**

Lfd. Nr.	Fahrgebiet / Route	Seetage	Seemeilen

Summe ________________ ________________

Übertrag

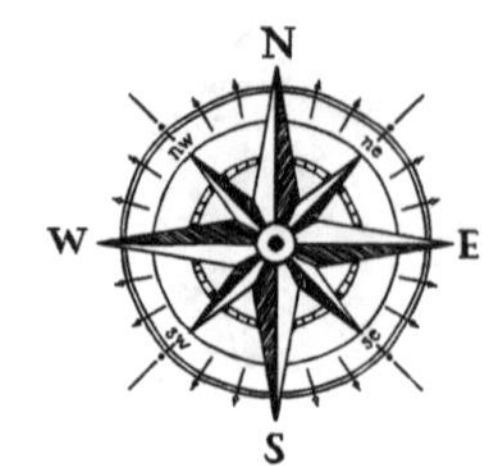

__________________ Seetage

__________________ Seemeilen

Lfd. Nr.	Fahrgebiet / Route	Seetage	Seemeilen

Summe __________________ __________________

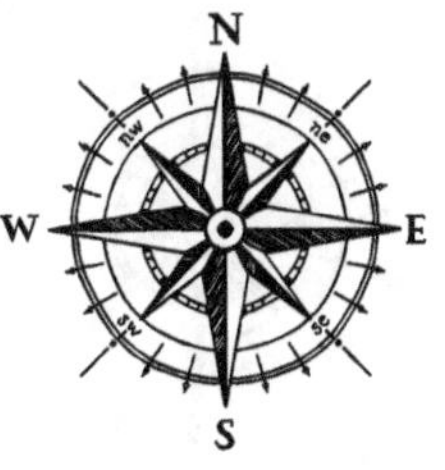

Übertrag

____
Seetage

____
Seemeilen

Lfd. Nr.	Fahrgebiet / Route	Seetage	Seemeilen

Summe ___________________ ___________________

Übertrag

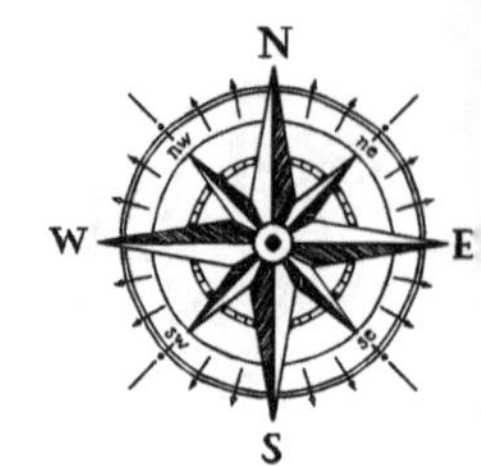

_______________   _______________
Seetage   **Seemeilen**

Lfd. Nr.	Fahrgebiet / Route	Seetage	Seemeilen

Summe _______________   _______________

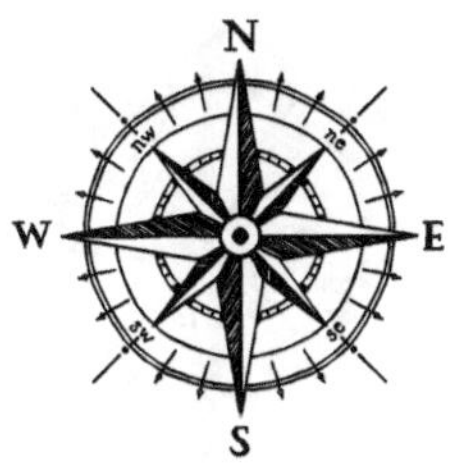

Übertrag

_______________________   _______________________

Seetage   **Seemeilen**

Lfd. Nr.	Fahrgebiet / Route	Seetage	Seemeilen

Summe _______________________ _______________________

Übertrag

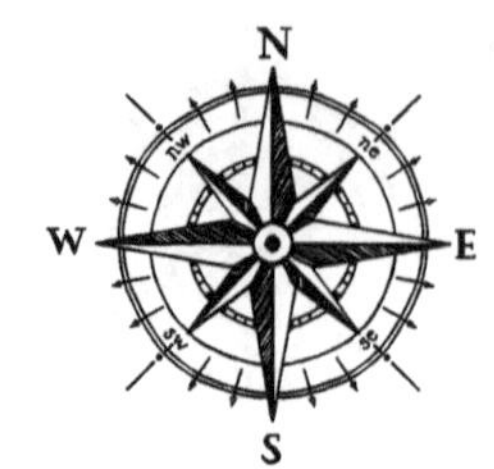

______________________   ______________________

    Seetage   **Seemeilen**

Lfd. Nr.	Fahrgebiet / Route	Seetage	Seemeilen

Summe ______________________   ______________________

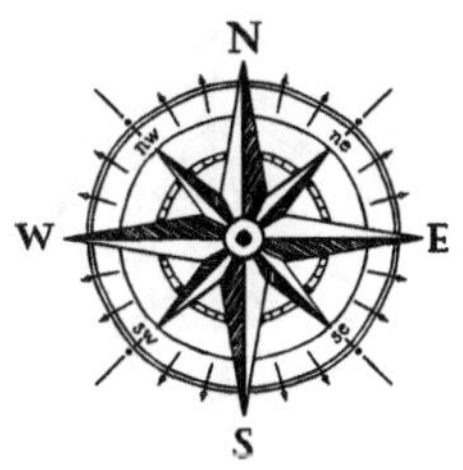

Übertrag

_______________________   _______________________

Seetage   **Seemeilen**

Lfd. Nr.	Fahrgebiet / Route	Seetage	Seemeilen

Summe _______________ _______________

Übertrag

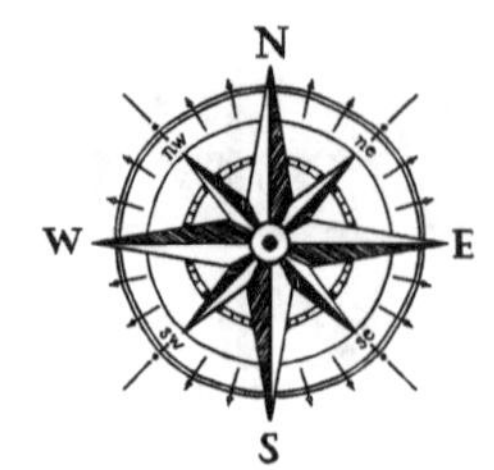

________________________   ________________________
Seetage   **Seemeilen**

Lfd. Nr.	Fahrgebiet / Route	Seetage	Seemeilen

Summe ________________ ________________

Übertrag

__________________________   __________________________

Seetage   **Seemeilen**

Lfd. Nr.	Fahrgebiet / Route	Seetage	Seemeilen

Summe __________________________ __________________________

Übertrag

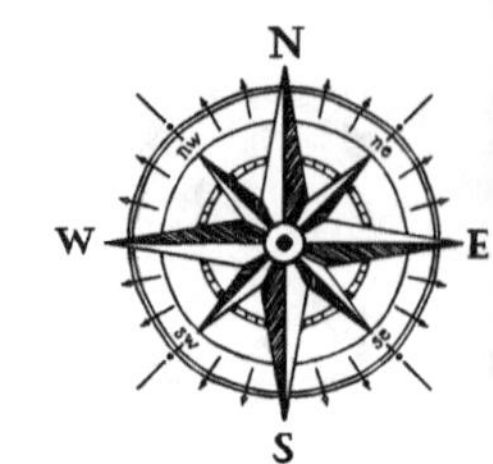

__________________ **Seetage**   __________________ **Seemeilen**

Lfd. Nr.	Fahrgebiet / Route	Seetage	Seemeilen

Summe __________________ __________________

Übertrag

_______________________   _______________________

Seetage   **Seemeilen**

Lfd. Nr.	Fahrgebiet / Route	Seetage	Seemeilen

Summe   _______________   _______________

Übertrag

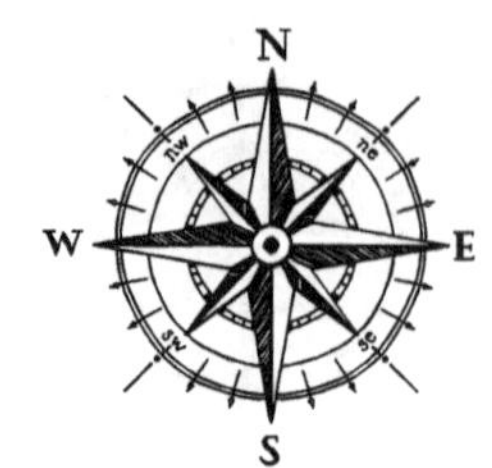

_______________   _______________

Seetage   **Seemeilen**

Lfd. Nr.	Fahrgebiet / Route	Seetage	Seemeilen

Summe   _______________   _______________

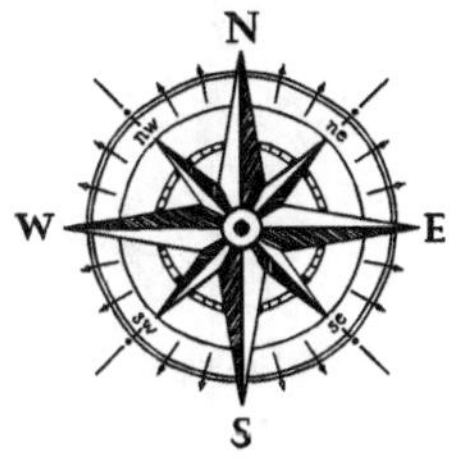

Übertrag

_______________________   _______________________

Seetage   **Seemeilen**

Lfd. Nr.	Fahrgebiet / Route	Seetage	Seemeilen

Summe   _______________________   _______________________

Übertrag

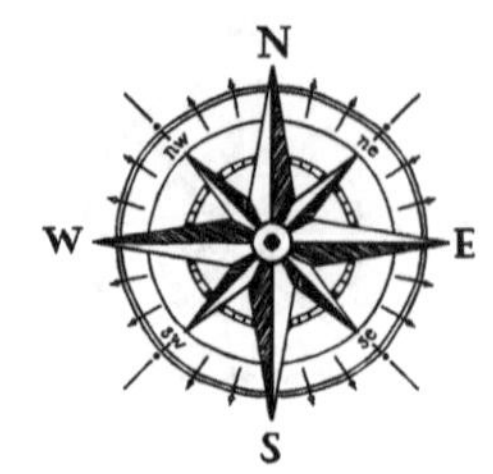

__________________________   __________________________
Seetage   **Seemeilen**

Lfd. Nr.	Fahrgebiet / Route	Seetage	Seemeilen

Summe   __________________   __________________